Welcome

We're happy you're here!

Please sign our guest book
&
share your experience with us
and future guests.

Guest Name/s: _____

Dates of My / Our Visit: _____ To _____ I / We Traveled From: _____

Reason for My / Our Trip: _____

Message To The Host: _____

_____

_____

Favorite Moments / Special Highlights of My / Our Stay

_____

_____

_____

_____

Places I/We Recommend - Restaurants - Entertainment - Must See Sights

_____

_____

_____

_____

Guest Name/s: _____

Dates of My / Our Visit: _____ To _____ I / We Traveled From: _____

Reason for My / Our Trip: _____

Message To The Host: _____

_____

_____

Favorite Moments / Special Highlights of My / Our Stay

_____

_____

_____

_____

Places I/We Recommend - Restaurants - Entertainment - Must See Sights

_____

_____

_____

_____

Guest Name/s: _____

Dates of My / Our Visit: _____ To _____ I / We Traveled From: _____

Reason for My / Our Trip: _____

Message To The Host: _____

_____

_____

Favorite Moments / Special Highlights of My / Our Stay

_____

_____

_____

_____

Places I/We Recommend - Restaurants - Entertainment - Must See Sights

_____

_____

_____

_____

Guest Name/s: _____

Dates of My / Our Visit: _____ To _____ I / We Traveled From: _____

Reason for My / Our Trip: _____

Message To The Host: _____

_____

_____

Favorite Moments / Special Highlights of My / Our Stay

_____

_____

_____

_____

Places I/We Recommend - Restaurants - Entertainment - Must See Sights

_____

_____

_____

_____

Guest Name/s: _____

Dates of My / Our Visit: _____ To _____ I / We Traveled From: _____

Reason for My / Our Trip: _____

Message To The Host: _____

_____

_____

Favorite Moments / Special Highlights of My / Our Stay

_____

_____

_____

_____

Places I/We Recommend - Restaurants - Entertainment - Must See Sights

_____

_____

_____

_____

Guest Name/s: _____

Dates of My / Our Visit: _____ To _____ I / We Traveled From: _____

Reason for My / Our Trip: _____

Message To The Host: _____

_____

_____

Favorite Moments / Special Highlights of My / Our Stay

_____

_____

_____

_____

Places I/We Recommend - Restaurants - Entertainment - Must See Sights

_____

_____

_____

_____

Guest Name/s: _____

Dates of My / Our Visit: _____ To _____ I / We Traveled From: _____

Reason for My / Our Trip: _____

Message To The Host: _____

_____

_____

Favorite Moments / Special Highlights of My / Our Stay

_____

_____

_____

_____

Places I / We Recommend - Restaurants - Entertainment - Must See Sights

_____

_____

_____

_____

Guest Name/s: _____

Dates of My / Our Visit: _____ To _____ I / We Traveled From: _____

Reason for My / Our Trip: _____

Message To The Host: _____

_____

_____

Favorite Moments / Special Highlights of My / Our Stay

_____

_____

_____

_____

Places I/We Recommend - Restaurants - Entertainment - Must See Sights

_____

_____

_____

_____

Guest Name/s: _____

Dates of My / Our Visit: _____ To _____ I / We Traveled From: _____

Reason for My / Our Trip: _____

Message To The Host: _____

_____

_____

Favorite Moments / Special Highlights of My / Our Stay

_____

_____

_____

_____

Places I/We Recommend - Restaurants - Entertainment - Must See Sights

_____

_____

_____

_____

Guest Name/s: _____

Dates of My / Our Visit: _____ To _____ I / We Traveled From: _____

Reason for My / Our Trip: _____

Message To The Host: _____

_____

_____

Favorite Moments / Special Highlights of My / Our Stay

_____

_____

_____

_____

Places I/We Recommend - Restaurants - Entertainment - Must See Sights

_____

_____

_____

_____

Guest Name/s: _____

Dates of My / Our Visit: _____ To _____ I / We Traveled From: _____

Reason for My / Our Trip: _____

Message To The Host: _____

_____

_____

Favorite Moments / Special Highlights of My / Our Stay

_____

_____

_____

_____

Places I / We Recommend - Restaurants - Entertainment - Must See Sights

_____

_____

_____

_____

Guest Name/s: _____

Dates of My / Our Visit: _____ To _____ I / We Traveled From: _____

Reason for My / Our Trip: _____

Message To The Host: _____

_____

_____

Favorite Moments / Special Highlights of My / Our Stay

_____

_____

_____

_____

Places I / We Recommend - Restaurants - Entertainment - Must See Sights

_____

_____

_____

_____

Guest Name/s: _____

Dates of My / Our Visit: _____ To _____ I / We Traveled From: _____

Reason for My / Our Trip: _____

Message To The Host: _____

_____

_____

Favorite Moments / Special Highlights of My / Our Stay

_____

_____

_____

_____

Places I / We Recommend - Restaurants - Entertainment - Must See Sights

_____

_____

_____

_____

Guest Name/s: _____

Dates of My / Our Visit: _____ To _____ I / We Traveled From: _____

Reason for My / Our Trip: _____

Message To The Host: _____

_____

_____

Favorite Moments / Special Highlights of My / Our Stay

_____

_____

_____

_____

Places I / We Recommend - Restaurants - Entertainment - Must See Sights

_____

_____

_____

_____

Guest Name/s: _____

Dates of My / Our Visit: _____ To _____ I / We Traveled From: _____

Reason for My / Our Trip: _____

Message To The Host: _____

_____

_____

Favorite Moments / Special Highlights of My / Our Stay

_____

_____

_____

_____

Places I / We Recommend - Restaurants - Entertainment - Must See Sights

_____

_____

_____

_____

Guest Name/s: _____

Dates of My / Our Visit: _____ To _____ I / We Traveled From: _____

Reason for My / Our Trip: _____

Message To The Host: _____

_____

_____

Favorite Moments / Special Highlights of My / Our Stay

_____

_____

_____

_____

Places I/We Recommend - Restaurants - Entertainment - Must See Sights

_____

_____

_____

_____

Guest Name/s: _____

Dates of My / Our Visit: _____ To _____ I / We Traveled From: _____

Reason for My / Our Trip: _____

Message To The Host: _____

_____

_____

Favorite Moments / Special Highlights of My / Our Stay

_____

_____

_____

_____

Places I / We Recommend - Restaurants - Entertainment - Must See Sights

_____

_____

_____

_____

Guest Name/s: _____

Dates of My / Our Visit: _____ To _____ I / We Traveled From: _____

Reason for My / Our Trip: _____

Message To The Host: _____

_____

_____

Favorite Moments / Special Highlights of My / Our Stay

_____

_____

_____

_____

Places I/We Recommend - Restaurants - Entertainment - Must See Sights

_____

_____

_____

_____

Guest Name/s: _____

Dates of My / Our Visit: _____ To _____ I / We Traveled From: _____

Reason for My / Our Trip: _____

Message To The Host: _____

_____

_____

Favorite Moments / Special Highlights of My / Our Stay

_____

_____

_____

_____

Places I / We Recommend - Restaurants - Entertainment - Must See Sights

_____

_____

_____

_____

Guest Name/s: _____

Dates of My / Our Visit: _____ To _____ I / We Traveled From: _____

Reason for My / Our Trip: _____

Message To The Host: _____

_____

_____

Favorite Moments / Special Highlights of My / Our Stay

_____

_____

_____

_____

Places I/We Recommend - Restaurants - Entertainment - Must See Sights

_____

_____

_____

_____

Guest Name/s: _____

Dates of My / Our Visit: _____ To _____ I / We Traveled From: _____

Reason for My / Our Trip: _____

Message To The Host: _____

_____

_____

Favorite Moments / Special Highlights of My / Our Stay

_____

_____

_____

_____

Places I/We Recommend - Restaurants - Entertainment - Must See Sights

_____

_____

_____

_____

Guest Name/s: _____

Dates of My / Our Visit: _____ To _____ I / We Traveled From: _____

Reason for My / Our Trip: _____

————————◆———————————◆————————

Message To The Host: _____

_____

_____

————————◆———————————◆————————

Favorite Moments / Special Highlights of My / Our Stay

_____

_____

_____

_____

————————◆———————————◆————————

Places I / We Recommend - Restaurants - Entertainment - Must See Sights

_____

_____

_____

_____

Guest Name/s: _____

Dates of My / Our Visit: _____ To _____ I / We Traveled From: _____

Reason for My / Our Trip: _____

Message To The Host: _____

_____

_____

Favorite Moments / Special Highlights of My / Our Stay

_____

_____

_____

_____

Places I / We Recommend - Restaurants - Entertainment - Must See Sights

_____

_____

_____

_____

Guest Name/s: _____

Dates of My / Our Visit: _____ To _____ I / We Traveled From: _____

Reason for My / Our Trip: _____

Message To The Host: _____

_____

_____

Favorite Moments / Special Highlights of My / Our Stay

_____

_____

_____

_____

Places I / We Recommend - Restaurants - Entertainment - Must See Sights

_____

_____

_____

_____

Guest Name/s: _____

Dates of My / Our Visit: _____ To _____ I / We Traveled From: _____

Reason for My / Our Trip: _____

Message To The Host: _____

_____

_____

Favorite Moments / Special Highlights of My / Our Stay

_____

_____

_____

_____

Places I/We Recommend - Restaurants - Entertainment - Must See Sights

_____

_____

_____

_____

Guest Name/s: _____

Dates of My / Our Visit: _____ To _____ I / We Traveled From: _____

Reason for My / Our Trip: _____

Message To The Host: _____

_____

_____

Favorite Moments / Special Highlights of My / Our Stay

_____

_____

_____

_____

Places I / We Recommend - Restaurants - Entertainment - Must See Sights

_____

_____

_____

_____

Guest Name/s: _____

Dates of My / Our Visit: _____ To _____ I / We Traveled From: _____

Reason for My / Our Trip: _____

Message To The Host: _____

_____

_____

Favorite Moments / Special Highlights of My / Our Stay

_____

_____

_____

_____

Places I / We Recommend - Restaurants - Entertainment - Must See Sights

_____

_____

_____

_____

Guest Name/s: _____

Dates of My / Our Visit: _____ To _____ I / We Traveled From: _____

Reason for My / Our Trip: _____

Message To The Host: _____

_____

_____

Favorite Moments / Special Highlights of My / Our Stay

_____

_____

_____

_____

Places I/We Recommend - Restaurants - Entertainment - Must See Sights

_____

_____

_____

_____

Guest Name/s: _____

Dates of My / Our Visit: _____ To _____ I / We Traveled From: _____

Reason for My / Our Trip: _____

Message To The Host: _____

_____

_____

Favorite Moments / Special Highlights of My / Our Stay

_____

_____

_____

_____

Places I / We Recommend - Restaurants - Entertainment - Must See Sights

_____

_____

_____

_____

Guest Name/s: _____

Dates of My / Our Visit: _____ To _____ I / We Traveled From: _____

Reason for My / Our Trip: _____

Message To The Host: _____

_____

_____

Favorite Moments / Special Highlights of My / Our Stay

_____

_____

_____

_____

Places I/We Recommend - Restaurants - Entertainment - Must See Sights

_____

_____

_____

_____

Guest Name/s: _____

Dates of My / Our Visit: _____ To _____ I / We Traveled From: _____

Reason for My / Our Trip: _____

Message To The Host: _____

_____

_____

Favorite Moments / Special Highlights of My / Our Stay

_____

_____

_____

_____

Places I/We Recommend - Restaurants - Entertainment - Must See Sights

_____

_____

_____

_____

Guest Name/s: _____

Dates of My / Our Visit: _____ To _____ I / We Traveled From: _____

Reason for My / Our Trip: _____

Message To The Host: _____

_____

_____

Favorite Moments / Special Highlights of My / Our Stay

_____

_____

_____

_____

Places I/We Recommend - Restaurants - Entertainment - Must See Sights

_____

_____

_____

_____

Guest Name/s: _____

Dates of My / Our Visit: _____ To _____ I / We Traveled From: _____

Reason for My / Our Trip: _____

Message To The Host: _____

_____

_____

Favorite Moments / Special Highlights of My / Our Stay

_____

_____

_____

_____

Places I/We Recommend - Restaurants - Entertainment - Must See Sights

_____

_____

_____

_____

Guest Name/s: _____

Dates of My / Our Visit: _____ To _____ I / We Traveled From: _____

Reason for My / Our Trip: _____

Message To The Host: _____

_____

_____

Favorite Moments / Special Highlights of My / Our Stay

_____

_____

_____

_____

Places I / We Recommend - Restaurants - Entertainment - Must See Sights

_____

_____

_____

_____

Guest Name/s: _____

Dates of My / Our Visit: _____ To _____ I / We Traveled From: _____

Reason for My / Our Trip: _____

❧ ————————————————————— ☙

Message To The Host: _____

_____

_____

❧ ————————————————————— ☙

Favorite Moments / Special Highlights of My / Our Stay

_____

_____

_____

_____

❧ ————————————————————— ☙

Places I /We Recommend - Restaurants - Entertainment - Must See Sights

_____

_____

_____

_____

Guest Name/s: _____

Dates of My / Our Visit: _____ To _____ I / We Traveled From: _____

Reason for My / Our Trip: _____

Message To The Host: _____

_____

_____

Favorite Moments / Special Highlights of My / Our Stay

_____

_____

_____

_____

Places I / We Recommend - Restaurants - Entertainment - Must See Sights

_____

_____

_____

_____

Guest Name/s: _____

Dates of My / Our Visit: _____ To _____ I / We Traveled From: _____

Reason for My / Our Trip: _____

Message To The Host: _____

_____

_____

Favorite Moments / Special Highlights of My / Our Stay

_____

_____

_____

_____

Places I / We Recommend - Restaurants - Entertainment - Must See Sights

_____

_____

_____

_____

Guest Name/s: _____

Dates of My / Our Visit: _____ To _____ I / We Traveled From: _____

Reason for My / Our Trip: _____

Message To The Host: _____

_____

_____

Favorite Moments / Special Highlights of My / Our Stay

_____

_____

_____

_____

Places I / We Recommend - Restaurants - Entertainment - Must See Sights

_____

_____

_____

_____

Guest Name/s: _____

Dates of My / Our Visit: _____ To _____ I / We Traveled From: _____

Reason for My / Our Trip: _____

Message To The Host: _____

_____

_____

Favorite Moments / Special Highlights of My / Our Stay

_____

_____

_____

_____

Places I/We Recommend - Restaurants - Entertainment - Must See Sights

_____

_____

_____

_____

Guest Name/s: _____

Dates of My / Our Visit: _____ To _____ I / We Traveled From: _____

Reason for My / Our Trip: _____

Message To The Host: _____

_____

_____

Favorite Moments / Special Highlights of My / Our Stay

_____

_____

_____

_____

Places I/We Recommend - Restaurants - Entertainment - Must See Sights

_____

_____

_____

_____

Guest Name/s: _____

Dates of My / Our Visit: _____ To _____ I / We Traveled From: _____

Reason for My / Our Trip: _____

Message To The Host: _____

_____

_____

Favorite Moments / Special Highlights of My / Our Stay

_____

_____

_____

_____

Places I / We Recommend - Restaurants - Entertainment - Must See Sights

_____

_____

_____

_____

Guest Name/s: _____

Dates of My / Our Visit: _____ To _____ I / We Traveled From: _____

Reason for My / Our Trip: _____

Message To The Host: _____

_____

_____

Favorite Moments / Special Highlights of My / Our Stay

_____

_____

_____

_____

Places I / We Recommend - Restaurants - Entertainment - Must See Sights

_____

_____

_____

_____

Guest Name/s: _____

Dates of My / Our Visit: _____ To _____ I / We Traveled From: _____

Reason for My / Our Trip: _____

Message To The Host: _____

_____

_____

Favorite Moments / Special Highlights of My / Our Stay

_____

_____

_____

_____

Places I/We Recommend - Restaurants - Entertainment - Must See Sights

_____

_____

_____

_____

Guest Name/s: _____

Dates of My / Our Visit: _____ To _____ I / We Traveled From: _____

Reason for My / Our Trip: _____

Message To The Host: _____

_____

_____

Favorite Moments / Special Highlights of My / Our Stay

_____

_____

_____

_____

Places I / We Recommend - Restaurants - Entertainment - Must See Sights

_____

_____

_____

_____

Guest Name/s: _____

Dates of My / Our Visit: _____ To _____ I / We Traveled From: _____

Reason for My / Our Trip: _____

Message To The Host: _____

_____

_____

Favorite Moments / Special Highlights of My / Our Stay

_____

_____

_____

_____

Places I/We Recommend - Restaurants - Entertainment - Must See Sights

_____

_____

_____

_____

Guest Name/s: _____

Dates of My / Our Visit: _____ To _____ I / We Traveled From: _____

Reason for My / Our Trip: _____

Message To The Host: _____

_____

_____

Favorite Moments / Special Highlights of My / Our Stay

_____

_____

_____

_____

Places I / We Recommend - Restaurants - Entertainment - Must See Sights

_____

_____

_____

_____

Guest Name/s: _____

Dates of My / Our Visit: _____ To _____ I / We Traveled From: _____

Reason for My / Our Trip: _____

Message To The Host: _____

_____

_____

Favorite Moments / Special Highlights of My / Our Stay

_____

_____

_____

_____

Places I/We Recommend - Restaurants - Entertainment - Must See Sights

_____

_____

_____

_____

Guest Name/s: _____

Dates of My / Our Visit: _____ To _____ I / We Traveled From: _____

Reason for My / Our Trip: _____

Message To The Host: _____

_____

_____

Favorite Moments / Special Highlights of My / Our Stay

_____

_____

_____

_____

Places I / We Recommend - Restaurants - Entertainment - Must See Sights

_____

_____

_____

_____

Guest Name/s: _____

Dates of My / Our Visit: _____ To _____ I / We Traveled From: _____

Reason for My / Our Trip: _____

❧ ——————————— ❧

Message To The Host: _____
_____
_____

❧ ——————————— ❧

Favorite Moments / Special Highlights of My / Our Stay

_____
_____
_____
_____

❧ ——————————— ❧

Places I / We Recommend - Restaurants - Entertainment - Must See Sights

_____
_____
_____
_____

Guest Name/s: _____

Dates of My / Our Visit: _____ To _____ I / We Traveled From: _____

Reason for My / Our Trip: _____

Message To The Host: _____

_____

_____

Favorite Moments / Special Highlights of My / Our Stay

_____

_____

_____

_____

Places I/We Recommend - Restaurants - Entertainment - Must See Sights

_____

_____

_____

_____

Guest Name/s: _____

Dates of My / Our Visit: _____ To _____ I / We Traveled From: _____

Reason for My / Our Trip: _____

Message To The Host: _____

_____

_____

Favorite Moments / Special Highlights of My / Our Stay

_____

_____

_____

_____

Places I / We Recommend - Restaurants - Entertainment - Must See Sights

_____

_____

_____

_____

Guest Name/s: _____

Dates of My / Our Visit: _____ To _____ I / We Traveled From: _____

Reason for My / Our Trip: _____

Message To The Host: _____

_____

_____

Favorite Moments / Special Highlights of My / Our Stay

_____

_____

_____

_____

Places I / We Recommend - Restaurants - Entertainment - Must See Sights

_____

_____

_____

_____

Guest Name/s: _____

Dates of My / Our Visit: _____ To _____ I / We Traveled From: _____

Reason for My / Our Trip: _____

Message To The Host: _____
_____
_____

Favorite Moments / Special Highlights of My / Our Stay

_____
_____
_____
_____

Places I/We Recommend - Restaurants - Entertainment - Must See Sights

_____
_____
_____
_____

Guest Name/s: _____

Dates of My / Our Visit: _____ To _____ I / We Traveled From: _____

Reason for My / Our Trip: _____

Message To The Host: _____

_____

_____

Favorite Moments / Special Highlights of My / Our Stay

_____

_____

_____

_____

Places I/We Recommend - Restaurants - Entertainment - Must See Sights

_____

_____

_____

_____

Guest Name/s: _____

Dates of My / Our Visit: _____ To _____ I / We Traveled From: _____

Reason for My / Our Trip: _____

Message To The Host: _____

_____

_____

Favorite Moments / Special Highlights of My / Our Stay

_____

_____

_____

_____

Places I/We Recommend - Restaurants - Entertainment - Must See Sights

_____

_____

_____

_____

Guest Name/s: _____

Dates of My / Our Visit: _____ To _____ I / We Traveled From: _____

Reason for My / Our Trip: _____

Message To The Host: _____

_____

_____

Favorite Moments / Special Highlights of My / Our Stay

_____

_____

_____

_____

Places I / We Recommend - Restaurants - Entertainment - Must See Sights

_____

_____

_____

_____

Guest Name/s: _____

Dates of My / Our Visit: _____ To _____ I / We Traveled From: _____

Reason for My / Our Trip: _____

Message To The Host: _____

_____

_____

Favorite Moments / Special Highlights of My / Our Stay

_____

_____

_____

_____

Places I / We Recommend - Restaurants - Entertainment - Must See Sights

_____

_____

_____

_____

Guest Name/s: _____

Dates of My / Our Visit: _____ To _____ I / We Traveled From: _____

Reason for My / Our Trip: _____

Message To The Host: _____

_____

_____

Favorite Moments / Special Highlights of My / Our Stay

_____

_____

_____

_____

Places I/We Recommend - Restaurants - Entertainment - Must See Sights

_____

_____

_____

_____

Guest Name/s: _____

Dates of My / Our Visit: _____ To _____ I / We Traveled From: _____

Reason for My / Our Trip: _____

Message To The Host: _____

_____

_____

Favorite Moments / Special Highlights of My / Our Stay

_____

_____

_____

_____

Places I/We Recommend - Restaurants - Entertainment - Must See Sights

_____

_____

_____

_____

Guest Name/s: _____

Dates of My / Our Visit: _____ To _____ I / We Traveled From: _____

Reason for My / Our Trip: _____

Message To The Host: _____

_____

_____

Favorite Moments / Special Highlights of My / Our Stay

_____

_____

_____

_____

Places I / We Recommend - Restaurants - Entertainment - Must See Sights

_____

_____

_____

_____

Guest Name/s: _____

Dates of My / Our Visit: _____ To _____ I / We Traveled From: _____

Reason for My / Our Trip: _____

Message To The Host: _____

_____

_____

Favorite Moments / Special Highlights of My / Our Stay

_____

_____

_____

_____

Places I / We Recommend - Restaurants - Entertainment - Must See Sights

_____

_____

_____

_____

Guest Name/s: _____

Dates of My / Our Visit: _____ To _____ I / We Traveled From: _____

Reason for My / Our Trip: _____

———————————— ✦ ————————————

Message To The Host: _____

_____

_____

———————————— ✦ ————————————

Favorite Moments / Special Highlights of My / Our Stay

_____

_____

_____

_____

———————————— ✦ ————————————

Places I/We Recommend - Restaurants - Entertainment - Must See Sights

_____

_____

_____

_____

Guest Name/s: _____

Dates of My / Our Visit: _____ To _____ I / We Traveled From: _____

Reason for My / Our Trip: _____

Message To The Host: _____

_____

_____

Favorite Moments / Special Highlights of My / Our Stay

_____

_____

_____

_____

Places I / We Recommend - Restaurants - Entertainment - Must See Sights

_____

_____

_____

_____

Guest Name/s: _____

Dates of My / Our Visit: _____ To _____ I / We Traveled From: _____

Reason for My / Our Trip: _____

Message To The Host: _____

_____

_____

Favorite Moments / Special Highlights of My / Our Stay

_____

_____

_____

_____

Places I/We Recommend - Restaurants - Entertainment - Must See Sights

_____

_____

_____

_____

Guest Name/s: _____

Dates of My / Our Visit: _____ To _____ I / We Traveled From: _____

Reason for My / Our Trip: _____

Message To The Host: _____

_____

_____

Favorite Moments / Special Highlights of My / Our Stay

_____

_____

_____

_____

Places I / We Recommend - Restaurants - Entertainment - Must See Sights

_____

_____

_____

_____

Guest Name/s: _____

Dates of My / Our Visit: _____ To _____ I / We Traveled From: _____

Reason for My / Our Trip: _____

Message To The Host: _____

_____

_____

Favorite Moments / Special Highlights of My / Our Stay

_____

_____

_____

_____

Places I/We Recommend - Restaurants - Entertainment - Must See Sights

_____

_____

_____

_____

Guest Name/s: _____

Dates of My / Our Visit: _____ To _____ I / We Traveled From: _____

Reason for My / Our Trip: _____

Message To The Host: _____

_____

_____

Favorite Moments / Special Highlights of My / Our Stay

_____

_____

_____

_____

Places I / We Recommend - Restaurants - Entertainment - Must See Sights

_____

_____

_____

_____

Guest Name/s: _____

Dates of My / Our Visit: _____ To _____ I / We Traveled From: _____

Reason for My / Our Trip: _____

Message To The Host: _____

_____

_____

Favorite Moments / Special Highlights of My / Our Stay

_____

_____

_____

_____

Places I/We Recommend - Restaurants - Entertainment - Must See Sights

_____

_____

_____

_____

Guest Name/s: _____

Dates of My / Our Visit: _____ To _____ I / We Traveled From: _____

Reason for My / Our Trip: _____

Message To The Host: _____

_____

_____

Favorite Moments / Special Highlights of My / Our Stay

_____

_____

_____

_____

Places I / We Recommend - Restaurants - Entertainment - Must See Sights

_____

_____

_____

_____

Guest Name/s: _____

Dates of My / Our Visit: _____ To _____ I / We Traveled From: _____

Reason for My / Our Trip: _____

———————— ⬗———————⬖ ————————

Message To The Host: _____

_____

_____

———————— ⬗———————⬖ ————————

Favorite Moments / Special Highlights of My / Our Stay

_____

_____

_____

_____

———————— ⬗———————⬖ ————————

Places I/We Recommend - Restaurants - Entertainment - Must See Sights

_____

_____

_____

_____

Guest Name/s: _____

Dates of My / Our Visit: _____ To _____ I / We Traveled From: _____

Reason for My / Our Trip: _____

Message To The Host: _____

_____

_____

Favorite Moments / Special Highlights of My / Our Stay

_____

_____

_____

_____

Places I/We Recommend - Restaurants - Entertainment - Must See Sights

_____

_____

_____

_____

Guest Name/s: _____

Dates of My / Our Visit: _____ To _____ I / We Traveled From: _____

Reason for My / Our Trip: _____

Message To The Host: _____

_____

_____

Favorite Moments / Special Highlights of My / Our Stay

_____

_____

_____

_____

Places I/We Recommend - Restaurants - Entertainment - Must See Sights

_____

_____

_____

_____

Guest Name/s: _____

Dates of My / Our Visit: _____ To _____ I / We Traveled From: _____

Reason for My / Our Trip: _____

Message To The Host: _____

_____

_____

Favorite Moments / Special Highlights of My / Our Stay

_____

_____

_____

_____

Places I/We Recommend - Restaurants - Entertainment - Must See Sights

_____

_____

_____

_____

Guest Name/s: _____

Dates of My / Our Visit: _____ To _____ I / We Traveled From: _____

Reason for My / Our Trip: _____

⊱—————————⊰

Message To The Host: _____

_____

_____

⊱—————————⊰

Favorite Moments / Special Highlights of My / Our Stay

_____

_____

_____

_____

⊱—————————⊰

Places I/We Recommend - Restaurants - Entertainment - Must See Sights

_____

_____

_____

_____

Guest Name/s: _____

Dates of My / Our Visit: _____ To _____ I / We Traveled From: _____

Reason for My / Our Trip: _____

Message To The Host: _____
_____
_____

Favorite Moments / Special Highlights of My / Our Stay

_____
_____
_____
_____

Places I/We Recommend - Restaurants - Entertainment - Must See Sights

_____
_____
_____
_____

Guest Name/s: _____

Dates of My / Our Visit: _____ To _____ I / We Traveled From: _____

Reason for My / Our Trip: _____

Message To The Host: _____

_____

_____

Favorite Moments / Special Highlights of My / Our Stay

_____

_____

_____

_____

Places I/We Recommend - Restaurants - Entertainment - Must See Sights

_____

_____

_____

_____

Guest Name/s: _____

Dates of My / Our Visit: _____ To _____ I / We Traveled From: _____

Reason for My / Our Trip: _____

Message To The Host: _____

_____

_____

Favorite Moments / Special Highlights of My / Our Stay

_____

_____

_____

_____

Places I/We Recommend - Restaurants - Entertainment - Must See Sights

_____

_____

_____

_____

Guest Name/s: _____

Dates of My / Our Visit: _____ To _____ I / We Traveled From: _____

Reason for My / Our Trip: _____

Message To The Host: _____

_____

_____

Favorite Moments / Special Highlights of My / Our Stay

_____

_____

_____

_____

Places I/We Recommend - Restaurants - Entertainment - Must See Sights

_____

_____

_____

_____

Guest Name/s: _____

Dates of My / Our Visit: _____ To _____ I / We Traveled From: _____

Reason for My / Our Trip: _____

Message To The Host: _____

_____

_____

Favorite Moments / Special Highlights of My / Our Stay

_____

_____

_____

_____

Places I/We Recommend - Restaurants - Entertainment - Must See Sights

_____

_____

_____

_____

Guest Name/s: _____

Dates of My / Our Visit: _____ To _____ I / We Traveled From: _____

Reason for My / Our Trip: _____

Message To The Host: _____

_____

_____

Favorite Moments / Special Highlights of My / Our Stay

_____

_____

_____

_____

Places I/We Recommend - Restaurants - Entertainment - Must See Sights

_____

_____

_____

_____

Guest Name/s: _____

Dates of My / Our Visit: _____ To _____ I / We Traveled From: _____

Reason for My / Our Trip: _____

Message To The Host: _____

_____

_____

Favorite Moments / Special Highlights of My / Our Stay

_____

_____

_____

_____

Places I/We Recommend - Restaurants - Entertainment - Must See Sights

_____

_____

_____

_____

Guest Name/s: _____

Dates of My / Our Visit: _____ To _____ I / We Traveled From: _____

Reason for My / Our Trip: _____

❦

Message To The Host: _____

_____

_____

❦

Favorite Moments / Special Highlights of My / Our Stay

_____

_____

_____

_____

❦

Places I/We Recommend - Restaurants - Entertainment - Must See Sights

_____

_____

_____

_____

Guest Name/s: _____

Dates of My / Our Visit: _____ To _____ I / We Traveled From: _____

Reason for My / Our Trip: _____

Message To The Host: _____

_____

_____

Favorite Moments / Special Highlights of My / Our Stay

_____

_____

_____

_____

Places I/We Recommend - Restaurants - Entertainment - Must See Sights

_____

_____

_____

_____

Guest Name/s: _____

Dates of My / Our Visit: _____ To _____ I / We Traveled From: _____

Reason for My / Our Trip: _____

—————————⟡—————————

Message To The Host: _____

_____

_____

—————————⟡—————————

Favorite Moments / Special Highlights of My / Our Stay

_____

_____

_____

_____

—————————⟡—————————

Places I/We Recommend - Restaurants - Entertainment - Must See Sights

_____

_____

_____

_____

Guest Name/s: _____

Dates of My / Our Visit: _____ To _____ I / We Traveled From: _____

Reason for My / Our Trip: _____

Message To The Host: _____

_____

_____

Favorite Moments / Special Highlights of My / Our Stay

_____

_____

_____

_____

Places I/We Recommend - Restaurants - Entertainment - Must See Sights

_____

_____

_____

_____

Guest Name/s: _____

Dates of My / Our Visit: _____ To _____ I / We Traveled From: _____

Reason for My / Our Trip: _____

Message To The Host: _____

_____

_____

Favorite Moments / Special Highlights of My / Our Stay

_____

_____

_____

_____

Places I/We Recommend - Restaurants - Entertainment - Must See Sights

_____

_____

_____

_____

Guest Name/s: _____

Dates of My / Our Visit: _____ To _____ I / We Traveled From: _____

Reason for My / Our Trip: _____

Message To The Host: _____

_____

_____

Favorite Moments / Special Highlights of My / Our Stay

_____

_____

_____

_____

Places I / We Recommend - Restaurants - Entertainment - Must See Sights

_____

_____

_____

_____

Guest Name/s: _____

Dates of My / Our Visit: _____ To _____ I / We Traveled From: _____

Reason for My / Our Trip: _____

Message To The Host: _____

_____

_____

Favorite Moments / Special Highlights of My / Our Stay

_____

_____

_____

_____

Places I/We Recommend - Restaurants - Entertainment - Must See Sights

_____

_____

_____

_____

Guest Name/s: _____

Dates of My / Our Visit: _____ To _____ I / We Traveled From: _____

Reason for My / Our Trip: _____

Message To The Host: _____

_____

_____

Favorite Moments / Special Highlights of My / Our Stay

_____

_____

_____

_____

Places I/We Recommend - Restaurants - Entertainment - Must See Sights

_____

_____

_____

_____

Guest Name/s: _____

Dates of My / Our Visit: _____ To _____ I / We Traveled From: _____

Reason for My / Our Trip: _____

Message To The Host: _____

_____

_____

Favorite Moments / Special Highlights of My / Our Stay

_____

_____

_____

_____

Places I/We Recommend - Restaurants - Entertainment - Must See Sights

_____

_____

_____

_____

Guest Name/s: _____

Dates of My / Our Visit: _____ To _____ I / We Traveled From: _____

Reason for My / Our Trip: _____

Message To The Host: _____

_____

_____

Favorite Moments / Special Highlights of My / Our Stay

_____

_____

_____

_____

Places I/We Recommend - Restaurants - Entertainment - Must See Sights

_____

_____

_____

_____

Guest Name/s: _____

Dates of My / Our Visit: _____ To _____ I / We Traveled From: _____

Reason for My / Our Trip: _____

Message To The Host: _____

_____

_____

Favorite Moments / Special Highlights of My / Our Stay

_____

_____

_____

_____

Places I / We Recommend - Restaurants - Entertainment - Must See Sights

_____

_____

_____

_____

Guest Name/s: _____

Dates of My / Our Visit: _____ To _____ I / We Traveled From: _____

Reason for My / Our Trip: _____

Message To The Host: _____

_____

_____

_____

Favorite Moments / Special Highlights of My / Our Stay

_____

_____

_____

_____

Places I / We Recommend - Restaurants - Entertainment - Must See Sights

_____

_____

_____

_____

Guest Name/s: _____

Dates of My / Our Visit: _____ To _____ I / We Traveled From: _____

Reason for My / Our Trip: _____

———◈——————◈———

Message To The Host: _____
_____
_____

———◈——————◈———

Favorite Moments / Special Highlights of My / Our Stay

_____
_____
_____
_____

———◈——————◈———

Places I/We Recommend - Restaurants - Entertainment - Must See Sights

_____
_____
_____
_____

Guest Name/s: _____

Dates of My / Our Visit: _____ To _____ I / We Traveled From: _____

Reason for My / Our Trip: _____

Message To The Host: _____

_____

_____

Favorite Moments / Special Highlights of My / Our Stay

_____

_____

_____

_____

Places I / We Recommend - Restaurants - Entertainment - Must See Sights

_____

_____

_____

_____

Guest Name/s: _____

Dates of My / Our Visit: _____ To _____ I / We Traveled From: _____

Reason for My / Our Trip: _____

Message To The Host: _____

_____

_____

Favorite Moments / Special Highlights of My / Our Stay

_____

_____

_____

_____

Places I/We Recommend - Restaurants - Entertainment - Must See Sights

_____

_____

_____

_____

Guest Name/s: _____

Dates of My / Our Visit: _____ To _____ I / We Traveled From: _____

Reason for My / Our Trip: _____

Message To The Host: _____

_____

_____

Favorite Moments / Special Highlights of My / Our Stay

_____

_____

_____

_____

Places I / We Recommend - Restaurants - Entertainment - Must See Sights

_____

_____

_____

_____

Guest Name/s: _____

Dates of My / Our Visit: _____ To _____ I / We Traveled From: _____

Reason for My / Our Trip: _____

⊱———————⊰

Message To The Host: _____

_____

_____

⊱———————⊰

Favorite Moments / Special Highlights of My / Our Stay

_____

_____

_____

_____

⊱———————⊰

Places I/We Recommend - Restaurants - Entertainment - Must See Sights

_____

_____

_____

_____

Guest Name/s: _____

Dates of My / Our Visit: _____ To _____ I / We Traveled From: _____

Reason for My / Our Trip: _____

Message To The Host: _____

_____

_____

Favorite Moments / Special Highlights of My / Our Stay

_____

_____

_____

_____

Places I/We Recommend - Restaurants - Entertainment - Must See Sights

_____

_____

_____

_____

Guest Name/s: _____

Dates of My / Our Visit: _____ To _____ I / We Traveled From: _____

Reason for My / Our Trip: _____

Message To The Host: _____

_____

_____

Favorite Moments / Special Highlights of My / Our Stay

_____

_____

_____

_____

Places I/We Recommend - Restaurants - Entertainment - Must See Sights

_____

_____

_____

_____

Guest Name/s: _____

Dates of My / Our Visit: _____ To _____ I / We Traveled From: _____

Reason for My / Our Trip: _____

Message To The Host: _____

_____

_____

Favorite Moments / Special Highlights of My / Our Stay

_____

_____

_____

_____

Places I / We Recommend - Restaurants - Entertainment - Must See Sights

_____

_____

_____

_____

Guest Name/s: _____

Dates of My / Our Visit: _____ To _____ I / We Traveled From: _____

Reason for My / Our Trip: _____

Message To The Host: _____

_____

_____

Favorite Moments / Special Highlights of My / Our Stay

_____

_____

_____

_____

Places I/We Recommend - Restaurants - Entertainment - Must See Sights

_____

_____

_____

_____

Guest Name/s: _____

Dates of My / Our Visit: _____ To _____ I / We Traveled From: _____

Reason for My / Our Trip: _____

Message To The Host: _____

_____

_____

Favorite Moments / Special Highlights of My / Our Stay

_____

_____

_____

_____

Places I / We Recommend - Restaurants - Entertainment - Must See Sights

_____

_____

_____

_____

Guest Name/s: _____

Dates of My / Our Visit: _____ To _____ I / We Traveled From: _____

Reason for My / Our Trip: _____

Message To The Host: _____

_____

_____

Favorite Moments / Special Highlights of My / Our Stay

_____

_____

_____

_____

Places I/We Recommend - Restaurants - Entertainment - Must See Sights

_____

_____

_____

_____

Guest Name/s: _____

Dates of My / Our Visit: _____ To _____ I / We Traveled From: _____

Reason for My / Our Trip: _____

Message To The Host: _____

_____

_____

_____

Favorite Moments / Special Highlights of My / Our Stay

_____

_____

_____

_____

Places I / We Recommend - Restaurants - Entertainment - Must See Sights

_____

_____

_____

_____

Guest Name/s: _____

Dates of My / Our Visit: _____ To _____ I / We Traveled From: _____

Reason for My / Our Trip: _____

Message To The Host: _____

_____

_____

Favorite Moments / Special Highlights of My / Our Stay

_____

_____

_____

_____

Places I / We Recommend - Restaurants - Entertainment - Must See Sights

_____

_____

_____

_____

Guest Name/s: _____

Dates of My / Our Visit: _____ To _____ I / We Traveled From: _____

Reason for My / Our Trip: _____

Message To The Host: _____

_____

_____

Favorite Moments / Special Highlights of My / Our Stay

_____

_____

_____

_____

Places I / We Recommend - Restaurants - Entertainment - Must See Sights

_____

_____

_____

_____

Guest Name/s: _____

Dates of My / Our Visit: _____ To _____ I / We Traveled From: _____

Reason for My / Our Trip: _____

Message To The Host: _____

_____

_____

Favorite Moments / Special Highlights of My / Our Stay

_____

_____

_____

_____

Places I/We Recommend - Restaurants - Entertainment - Must See Sights

_____

_____

_____

_____

Guest Name/s: _____

Dates of My / Our Visit: _____ To _____ I / We Traveled From: _____

Reason for My / Our Trip: _____

Message To The Host: _____

_____

_____

Favorite Moments / Special Highlights of My / Our Stay

_____

_____

_____

_____

Places I/We Recommend - Restaurants - Entertainment - Must See Sights

_____

_____

_____

_____

Guest Name/s: _____

Dates of My / Our Visit: _____ To _____ I / We Traveled From: _____

Reason for My / Our Trip: _____

Message To The Host: _____

_____

_____

Favorite Moments / Special Highlights of My / Our Stay

_____

_____

_____

_____

Places I/We Recommend - Restaurants - Entertainment - Must See Sights

_____

_____

_____

_____

Made in the USA
Columbia, SC
08 September 2024

41995959R00063